HOW CAN I HELP?

Roly
the
hedgehog

Frances Rodgers and **Ben Grisdale**

Penguin
Random
House

Written and illustrated by
Frances Rodgers and Ben Grisdale

Editor Abi Luscombe
Project Art Editor Charlotte Bull
Managing Editor Laura Gilbert
Publishing Manager Francesca Young
Publishing Coordinator Issy Walsh
Production Editor Dragana Puvacic
Production Controller Isabell Schart
Deputy Art Director Mabel Chan
Publishing Director Sarah Larter

First published in Great Britain in 2021
by Dorling Kindersley Limited
DK, One Embassy Gardens,
8 Viaduct Gardens, London, SW11 7BW

The authorised representative in the EEA is
Dorling Kindersley Verlag GmbH. Arnulfstr.
124, 80636 Munich, Germany

For the curious
www.dk.com

MIX
Paper from
responsible sources
FSC™ C018179

This book was made with Forest Stewardship
Council™ certified paper - one small step
in DK's commitment to a sustainable future.

For more information go to
www.dk.com/our-green-pledge

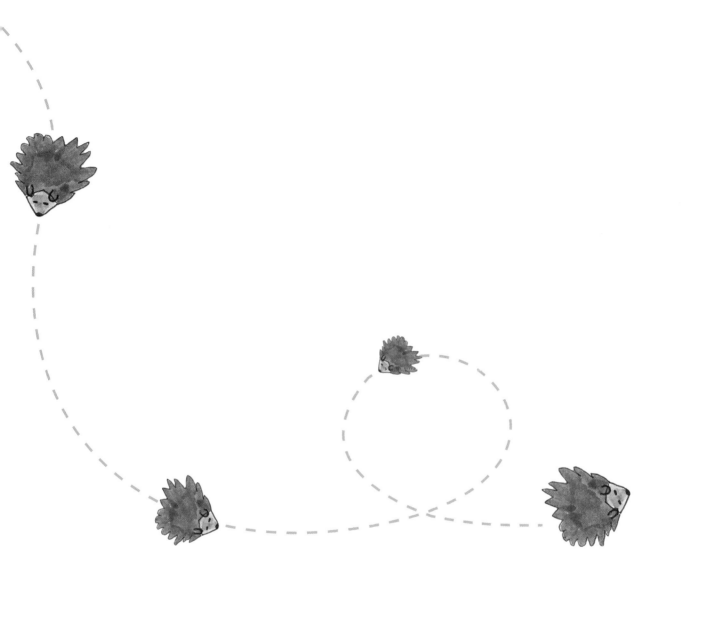

Hello, my name is Roly.
I am a hedgehog and I like
to visit your garden.
But I need your help.

Please let me into your garden. Ask a grownup to make me a doorway in your fence.

12 cm (5 in)

I like to eat things that I can
find in your garden.

Please plant flowers to attract the slugs and bugs.

I get very thirsty.

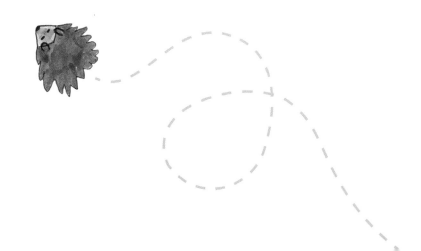

**Please leave a small
bowl of water out for me**.

I can get stuck in rubbish.

Please keep your garden tidy.

Bin

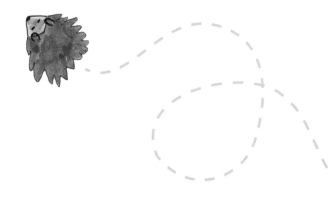

Ponds can be a danger to me.

**Please give me a ladder
in case I fall in.**

I can also get stuck in nets.

**Please lift them up
when not in use**.

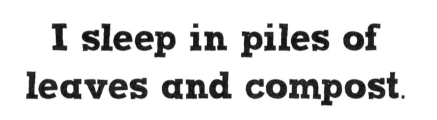

I sleep in piles of
leaves and compost.

Please be careful and look for me
before you clear them up.

Thank you for all your help.

Why do we need to protect hedgehogs?

Hedgehogs like Roly need to be protected. Hedgehogs are found in Europe, Asia, Africa, and New Zealand but there are not many of them left in the world.

Scientists are worried that these little animals will go extinct soon, which means that they won't exist any more, because they are struggling to find places to sleep and enough food to eat.

It is up to us to do what we can to help!

Prickly protection

Spines

Newborn hedgehogs are called hoglets. When they are born, hoglets have a few soft, white spines covering their wrinkly, pink bodies. As they grow up, their spines become sharper, harder, and longer.

Hoglet

Fully grown hedgehogs can have as many as 7,000 spines!

These spines can come in handy when these small animals are in danger. When they get scared or when they are sleeping, they curl up into a prickly ball.

When they are curled up, hedgehogs look a bit like pine cones. This protects the soft parts of their body, such as their tail, face, belly, and legs.

Can you see any hedgehog pine cones in your garden?

Hibernation

Hedgehogs are very dozy creatures who spend a lot of their life asleep. Some hedgehogs can sleep for up to 18 hours a day and need to hibernate (rest) through the chilly winter months.

Hibernation is when animals, including some hedgehogs, go into a deep sleep because the weather is too cold and it is hard to find food. But before they hibernate they must gather lots of food.

Caterpillars

Earwigs

Unfortunately, these spiny creatures don't have very good eyesight so they have to use their hearing and their long snout to hunt creatures such as slugs and caterpillars.

Earthworms

Slugs

Millipedes

When they are out looking for food, hedgehogs can walk for up to 2 miles (3 km) – that's a long way for little legs!

Yum!

Acknowledgements

The publisher would like to thank the following for their kind permission to reproduce their photographs:

(Key: a-above; b-below/bottom; c-centre; f-far; l-left; r-right; t-top)

34 Dreamstime.com: Cynoclub (cl); Eric Isselee (cr).
35 Dreamstime.com: Eric Isselee (bl). **39 Dorling Kindersley:** Natural History Museum, London (clb). **Getty Images:** Photographer's Choice RF / Jon Boyes

All other images © Dorling Kindersley
For further information see: www.dkimages.com

About the author and illustrator

Ben and Frances are husband and wife and they live in Newcastle upon Tyne, England. They are passionate about helping the wildlife in their garden. In the middle of a summer's night, Frances woke with an idea to create books to encourage young children to do the same.

Frances wrote the books and Ben illustrated them and they brought to life *Roly the hedgehog*, *Rory the garden bird*, *Rosy the bumblebee*, and *Roxy the butterfly*.